AWESOME DOGS

French Bulldogs

by Mari Schuh

BLASTOFF!
2
READERS

BELLWETHER MEDIA • MINNEAPOLIS, MN

Note to Librarians, Teachers, and Parents:

Blastoff! Readers are carefully developed by literacy experts and combine standards-based content with developmentally appropriate text.

Level 1 provides the most support through repetition of high-frequency words, light text, predictable sentence patterns, and strong visual support.

Level 2 offers early readers a bit more challenge through varied simple sentences, increased text load, and less repetition of high-frequency words.

Level 3 advances early-fluent readers toward fluency through increased text and concept load, less reliance on visuals, longer sentences, and more literary language.

Level 4 builds reading stamina by providing more text per page, increased use of punctuation, greater variation in sentence patterns, and increasingly challenging vocabulary.

Level 5 encourages children to move from "learning to read" to "reading to learn" by providing even more text, varied writing styles, and less familiar topics.

Whichever book is right for your reader, Blastoff! Readers are the perfect books to build confidence and encourage a love of reading that will last a lifetime!

This edition first published in 2016 by Bellwether Media, Inc.

No part of this publication may be reproduced in whole or in part without written permission of the publisher. For information regarding permission, write to Bellwether Media, Inc., Attention: Permissions Department, 5357 Penn Avenue South, Minneapolis, MN 55419.

Library of Congress Cataloging-in-Publication Data

Schuh, Mari C., 1975- author.
  French Bulldogs / by Mari Schuh.
     pages cm. – (Blastoff! Readers. Awesome Dogs)
  Summary: "Relevant images match informative text in this introduction to French bulldogs. Intended for students in kindergarten through third grade"– Provided by publisher.
  Audience: Ages 5-8
  Audience: K to grade 3
  Includes bibliographical references and index.
  ISBN 978-1-62617-239-5 (hardcover: alk. paper)
  1. French bulldog–Juvenile literature. I. Title.
  SF429.F8S38 2016
  636.7'2–dc23
                              2015009732

Printed in the United States of America, North Mankato, MN.

Table of
Contents

What Are French Bulldogs?

French bulldogs are powerful little dogs. They are cheerful and **alert**.

These charming dogs like to play.
But they are strong-willed.

French bulldogs have big,
square heads and short noses.
Their ears look like bat ears.

Wrinkles cover their faces and shoulders.

French bulldogs have wide, powerful bodies. Their legs are short and strong.

French Bulldog Profile

bat-like ears —

big, square head

wrinkled face and shoulders

— short, strong legs

Life Span: 11 to 13 years

Trainability:

| 1 | 2 | 3 | 4 | 5 | 6 |

Hardest to train   Easiest to train

These dogs can weigh up to 28 pounds (13 kilograms).

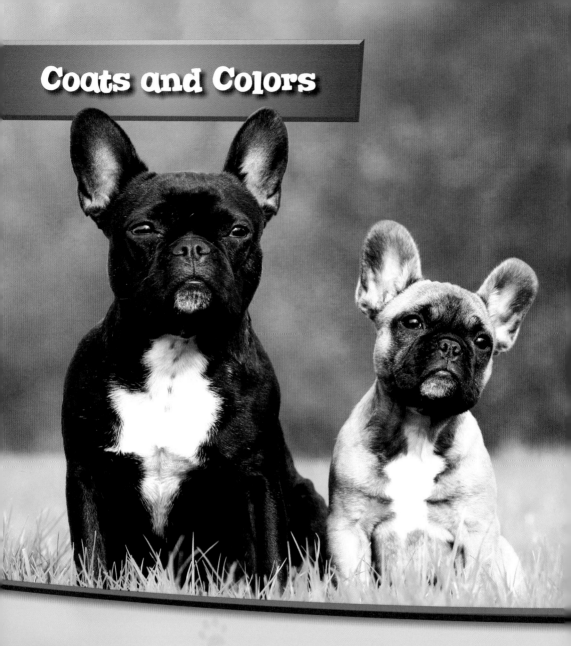

French bulldogs have short **coats**. They are smooth and shiny.

French Bulldog Coats

brindle   white   fawn

Coat colors include **brindle**, white, and **fawn**. Coats can be one or two colors.

History of French Bulldogs

French bulldogs actually came from England. In the 1800s, small English bulldogs kept workers company.

England

France

N
W E
S

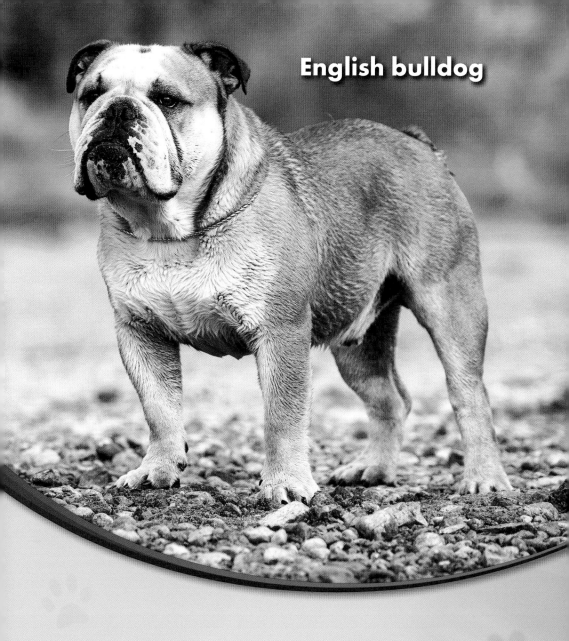

English bulldog

Later, some workers moved to France. They brought their small bulldogs with them.

The bulldogs had puppies with other **breeds** in France. These puppies became French bulldogs.

The **American Kennel Club** now puts the breed in its **Non-Sporting Group**.

Playful and Cuddly

French bulldogs rarely bark. But they are good watchdogs. They will bark if they sense danger.

These popular pets are noisy in other ways. They snore and **wheeze**.

Hot weather bothers French
bulldogs. They mostly stay indoors.

Still, they play outside a little.
They enjoy short walks.

French bulldogs are
fun and friendly.

These sweet dogs enjoy being around people. They love to cuddle and sleep on laps!

Glossary

alert—quick to notice or act

American Kennel Club—an organization that keeps track of dog breeds in the United States

breeds—types of dogs

brindle—a solid coat color mixed with streaks or spots of another color

coats—the hair or fur covering some animals

fawn—a light brown color

Non-Sporting Group—a group of dog breeds that do not usually hunt or work

wheeze—to have a hard time breathing

wrinkles—lines in skin or fur

To Learn More

AT THE LIBRARY
Barnes, Nico. *Bulldogs*. Minneapolis, Minn.: Abdo Kids, 2015.

DiPucchio, Kelly. *Gaston*. New York, N.Y.: Atheneum Books for Young Readers, 2014.

Rustad, Martha E. H. *Dogs*. North Mankato, Minn.: Capstone Press, 2015.

ON THE WEB
Learning more about
French bulldogs
is as easy as 1, 2, 3.

1. Go to www.factsurfer.com.

2. Enter "French bulldogs" into the search box.

3. Click the "Surf" button and you will see a list of related web sites.

With factsurfer.com, finding more information is just a click away.

Index